MW00955823

Hold your form.

Emotional Intelligence in its simplest form.

Sharyn Combs, CHBC, CRCST
UCDI Leadership
Do Something Daily, LLC.

Hold your form.

ISBN 978-0-359-91319-0

CSYX Solutions

DSD Enterprises, 4011 Shilling Way, Dallas, TX 75237. Printed in the USA.

"Be You"

Hey! Be you. Be authentically you. No one can be you better than you can be you and you'll never be able to be anybody else. So why waste that time? You are fearfully and wonderfully made. Actually, you are tailor made. You are your own designer style, *so be you*. People love you. You. They don't want an imitation of you, and they do not want an invitation to be someone else coming through you. The purpose of this writing is to encourage you to THINK. on Purpose, Hold. Your. Form. and be yourself.

When it's all said and done, being you is liberating. That is simply the best word for it. Liberating. It's liberating to be yourself; to be free. Be You. Enjoy life. Focus on your goals. Focus on the things you want to see, to improve, and just, you know, *be the best you that you can be*. It is absolutely okay to do so.

PLEASE NOTE: In order to be the TRUE you, you must get to know yourself.

Contents

Thank you. 5

"Get Them, Wind!" 6

Finish the Drill. 9

Progressive Progress 13

Dead Conversations, Dead Endeavors 20

Failure and Disappointment 27

Overwhelm-ness 37

Going LEAN... 42

Why 'Hold Your Form?' 46

Coach's Talk 51

Excerpts from Real Conversations 53

Thank you.

To Brenda and Kathy and Ronda and Donnie, to Cindy and Sandi and Cortez and Mathman aka Alester Givens, to Cynthia and Lauren and the other Kathy and Angela, to Scott and Dee and Howard and Amy and Doug…for some reason I want to write 'Ronnie, Bobbie, Ricky and Mike- if I love the girl who cares who you like!" Ahhh, humor. ☐ Thanks to all of my friends who support and encourage me (and UCDI/Do Something Daily), thank you to radio hosts and event planners. Thank you to T-shirt wearers, bracelet rockers, gap standers and 'dipped in pockets.' I appreciate you all.

And now, for THE most important thanks of this endeavor; Thank You, Lord. For Your patience, Your grace, Your mercy and longsuffering. For allowing me to have a sound mind and experience things in my life that I didn't even know to dream for. At my best and at my worst, my heart is forever Yours.

Chapter 1

"Get Them, Wind!"

Endurance will beat and outlast enthusiasm every single time.

A few years back my nephew Timothy played football and he could run a 40-meter dash in 4.3 seconds. He was fast and very proficient in athletics. During Tim's junior year in high school, his coach suggested that my nephew run track to enhance his football skills. Tim agreed, and almost immediately, he was placed on the varsity track team. After a few races and a few wins, the competition became more stiff and the track coaches assigned him to run a longer distance. The 400 meters. Tim readily accepted.

As usual and because Tim was already athletically competent, he was confident that he could do this greater distance with ease. Although I did not see the race, my sister told me it went something like this: Tim lined up as he usually lined up after stretching as he usually stretched. He came out of the starters block as he usually did-fast; and took the lead as he usually did. And this is where 'the usual' stopped.

The 400-meter race is one full lap and the distance is equivalent to one quarter of a mile. My sister said that about the third curve of this lap- this one FULL lap- she said she could tell something was different with Tim's stride. She could see he was having some challenges and was not able to run as he usually ran. The other runners began to pass him. After the race she asked him what happened; "I don't know what happened," he said, "I was running as hard as I could. I saw them passing me and I was like, 'Get them wind. *Get them!*'" The wind had begun to work against him because he could no longer hold his form. His conditioning and his endurance were still 40-yard dash-ish. Tim not prepared himself for the more demanding race.

M.L. Rose writes: "...not even the world's elite runners can run a full 400 meters at top speed. If you try, you'll likely run out of gas too soon and the field will fly by you. (How to Pace Yourself for a 400-Meter Dash)." As proficient an athlete as Tim was, he lacked the skill and endurance necessary to be successful at *this next level*. Note: he did not lack the talent or ability. The raw materials were there. He lacked the endurance and skill that accompanies preparation. Tim approached both races as if they were the same and in so doing, he failed to prepare for the assignment his coaches gave him. As a result, he wasn't able to hold his form. His elbows began to get out of sorts, further away from his body; his legs didn't have the height associated with running a longer distance, his head was too high, his chin was not tucked in- everything was out of alignment. He was unable to perform optimally and get the victory to which he was accustomed. There are times in your life when enthusiasm will not get the job done. You must have endurance; you must have conditioning.

There are times in your life when enthusiasm will not get the job done. You must have endurance; you must have conditioning.

My nephew Tim was unable to hold his form in the 400-meter race. And it resulted in a loss where he was accustomed to winning. Many times, in professional growth or promotion we try to force past methodologies into new spaces. In the 40-yard dash, the best tactic is to START with a burst of speed, in the 400 meter you END with your best sprint. In order to hold your form, you must know the form you are holding.

Chapter TWO

Finish the Drill.

"Do You Know Your Form?"

During the basketball season I get an opportunity to officiate basketball. There will be times when the players are playing and something occurs- they may make a mistake, or they may think that a foul should be called, or they may think that a violation should be called- and they will just stop. They simply stop moving- but no one has blown the whistle.

The most amazing type of this occurrence (to me) is when it is in a one-and-one free throw situation. When it's a one-and-one, the offensive team gets to shoot a free shot at the basket. If they make the shot, they get another shot. If they miss the shot, you just get the rebound and normal play resumes. Periodically, what will happen is the shooter will miss the first shot, a player will get the rebound and because no one else is moving, the player with the ball will just stop.

No one has blown the whistle. No one has done anything; the person with the ball (i.e. *the opportunity*) just stopped and ended up committing a violation. THEY lost the ball *because they just stopped.* Amazingly, people engage in this madness too... they just stop. Just stopping is not limited to sports; it happens in relationships, life, careers- it happens in many places. There is a quote that I have heard many times among peak performers that states:

"Most people die at age 30, they just wait another fifty years to get buried." They just stop. You don't want to just stop; *finish*. Finish the drill, finish the task, finish what you've begun. Things will come for your attention. Things will come for your money. Things will come for that creative energy that you are investing in your endeavors. But hold your form and finish it up. Understand that when you begin to move towards something and focus, truly focus on a desired end, things will come for that focus. Hold your form. It may even seem like your end goal is getting further away but it is not. When you begin to move towards something, you are covering ground and gaining traction. You're making progress.

No one stopped them, they just stopped themselves.

Personal growth leads to professional growth. If you have personal growth, you will have professional growth. However, when you have professional growth without personal growth, your professional growth will not be sustainable, and it will eat away at your core. *Personal growth is essential for a healthy quality of life.* Professional growth requires personal growth for emotional intelligence to support business and career needs. The growth needs to be commensurate, conducive, and able to handle the weight of the responsibilities that you're growing into within your respective frameworks- your mental framework, your emotional and spiritual framework, your EQ, your emotional intelligence-even relational equity frameworks. You must commit to the growth to get the returns you desire. This commitment allows you to hold your form when you would otherwise quit or give up. When you commit to personal growth, you become more self-aware and are no longer at the mercy of external circumstances. You are now able to finish the tasks, finish the drills and charge toward the very destinations you have charted.

Many times, while speaking or conducting training, my audiences will share with me that they have a plan. To write a book, to start a business, to get into investing, etc. However, within two to three questions, that plan is breaking down and it turns out that it is not a plan at all. Please know, that when I ask my audience these questions, they are never to discourage, or place shame and anxiety on anyone in the audience. On the contrary, the questions are asked to position the person for success. Here's the thing, we want to count the cost beforehand. We want to be able to make informed decisions within the market, with our finances, and with the relationships of those that are connected to us. For a higher probability of success, you will want to count all known costs associated with your projects. I recommend including a percentage for unforeseen costs also. You don't want to get out in the middle of the ocean and find out that your boat only has gas for half of the trip or find out that your boat is not built for the size of the waves. Count the costs beforehand. When people are telling me their plans and what they want to do and what they want to have, I ask these questions. Then I know whether they actually have a plan, or whether this is still an idea in their mind.

An idea is not synonymous with a plan. The first without the second is a pipe dream, or a nightmare...

If you don't know how to finish, you will think because you have an idea that you have a plan. An idea is not synonymous with a plan. The first without the second is a pipe dream-or a nightmare because it will torment the dreamer. An idea helps you know your form; the plan helps you finish.

Chapter THREE

Progressive Progress

TIPS to MOVE the Needle Forward

Progressive Practice Tip 1:
Be S.M.A.R.T.

Often when people make goals, they only think of changes they will need to make. If you are familiar with SMART goals, you know that a goal, any goal, is more than just what 'I' am going to do, or how 'I' am going to do it. S.M.A.R.T. goals are more than just specific because what 'I' am going to do is only a percentage of what is needed to accomplish any goal. In addition to being specific, S.M.A.R.T. goals are measurable, attainable/achievable, relevant and time bound. To help move the needle forward, let's go over a few strategies to help with goals.

Many people start plans, implement plans, and even announce plans, but without a strategic and tactical approach, the newness wears off and it becomes yet another rock on the mountain of unfulfilled dreams. I want to encourage you to keep going for sustained success. Don't vacillate, don't go high and then go low. Just keep going. *Make constant and consistent steps* towards your progress. You will reach your goal; just make it S.M.A.R.T.

1.Specific
2. Measurable

3. Achievable
4. Relevant,
5. Time bound.

Once your goal is S.M.A.R.T., you now have <u>a</u> <u>track to run on</u>. You have a timeline. You will want to ensure you give yourself enough time to walk out the completion of your goals; not just the whole goal, but each part of the goal. For example, if one part of an improved communication goal is to get members of your team to practice communicating using a certain method in a shift change huddle, then give yourself (*and your team*) time to repeatedly use that improvement method.

How does that look? Like this:

"For one to two weeks, I'm going to implement this new practice of verbally communicating in a huddle with the oncoming and off-going staff, asking the huddle members to repeat what they've heard, and then asking the huddle members if they have everything they need for the case schedule, and if there is anything I can do to make their job easier. This new interactive method will replace the top down, one-way communication flow where one person talks and relays the information for the upcoming shift."

Although that is just one example, it demonstrates that goals, especially career and professional goals, often include more than the 'I' mentioned earlier. If your goal includes people other than yourself, you will want to give *time*. You <u>must</u> give time. Time allows you, (and others), to see how the method is working, how it is not working, where it is working, where it is not, etc. You will want to follow a process; the simpler the process, the better.

For day-to-day processes, I recommend bite sized actions. Give yourself small to medium steps. Don't make your first goal taking over the world. Before you take over the world, take over a continent. Before you take over a continent, you might need to take over a country. Before you take over a country, take over a state, a city, a neighborhood, a house...*you*. Confirm you have a handle on yourself before you demand others conform to your ideals. But I digress, and you can learn more about that in my book "*THINK. On Purpose*."

The benefits of having progressive goals are that they lead towards your larger goals and allow you to have experience meeting and achieving deliverables. They provide experience with timelines and adjustments- when to adjust and when not to adjust. Smaller goals allow you to track your progress more effectively.

Progressive Practice Tip 2:
The Color Code

Place your plan on a calendar. Use colors to color code the calendar, so you (and your team) can see what is complete, what needs to be completed, and which deadline is approaching. Colors provide a visual consistency tracker. I used the color green for consistency. So, if I look at my calendar and I see that I have five days that are green, but then suddenly, I have three that are not, I know that I need to get back on track.

The visual consistency tracker indicates when you may be getting lax in moving toward your goals. Make the calendar your friend, make the calendar work for you. Track your progress. Another thing that helps keep moving the needle forward is to find role models and inspirational stories. Look back at times you've been successful and use those stories to motivate you and inspire you to keep going. When you're in the day to day, sometimes you can forget your why, and things may seem overwhelming or far off. Inspirational stories can help remind you of the inevitability of success.

The only thing keeping you from what you really want is the story you keep telling yourself about why you do not have it yet. -Tony Robbins

Stories help me when I get caught up in the day to day routine. It happens- you're tired, you're frustrated, you haven't had a day off. You're working with others and it seems as if your productivity is twice their productivity. At those times, you have to make a conscious choice not to get burnt out, not to give in to apathy, and not to give up on your goals. You must hold your form and not allow cynical and negative behavior to influence your goals. *Find your inspirational story, find your role model, and keep your goals, your goals.*

Let these things inspire you and influence you; not the negative or counterproductive behaviors you may see. Get involved with groups. I myself am part of a lovely group on Facebook; we talk about thought processes, cognition, and share encouraging tips with one another. There are all kinds of groups that you can surround yourself with. People who are peak performers, people who are visionaries, people who keep you accountable, who inspire you to keep pushing, to reach your goals. So, get involved with groups. If that means you must step out of your comfort zone for just a moment to meet someone, go ahead and do that. It's only uncomfortable now because you haven't done it. Remember the first time you had to swim or drive by yourself. It was a little uncomfortable, but it was only because it was something you did not have a lot of experience with. But now that you've been doing it awhile, it gets more comfortable- *and you get more confident.*

Get involved, stay engaged. Your confidence and your competency will improve. Talk about your goals with people who do- and who do not- support you in the journey. People who do support you are energizing; and it's going to be organic and life giving between both the giver and receiver. When you begin to speak your goals you feel encouraged, inspired, and motivated, like: "Let's do this. We can make it happen." And *you begin to move* toward your goals.

It even helps you when you talk about your goals with people who aren't supporting you in your journey. Because it keeps that conversation, *and the accompanying misplaced energy,* minimal. Some individuals are just disgruntled and toxic. Talking about your goals with these individuals help you recognize cynical, embittered and stagnant key words. It gives you practice navigating negative conversations.

It protects you. So talk. Talk about your goals with people who do and don't support you. However, do not waste time and emotion trying to prove someone wrong, that means you are focused more on them than on you and *they have become your driver.* Understand most people are not going to be as passionate about your vision as you are. That's normal. It's okay. Keep going. They're going to be times when you feel discouraged, afraid, and even alone. Just keep moving. If you follow the steps, you will reach the goals you've set. Being consistent doesn't mean you have to be perfect. Don't try to be perfect. That's a very heavy load. Just be consistent.

Chapter 4

Dead Conversations, Dead Endeavors

Being Intentional with our Tongue

There is an old gambler's song by Kenny Rogers that goes, "you have to know when the hold 'em...know when to fold 'em. Know when to walk away and know when to run..." You must know this principle in business and in navigating promotion. When I was younger, if someone asked me to define success, I would use language such as money, cars, houses, even clothing. But my younger definition was born out of a deficit. Success is relative and holistic; meaning it is internal and external. My younger definition was solely external. Not only was it external, it was not connected to my passion, my promise or my purpose. To be clear: I am not negating those external items in the least- we all need money, transportation and shelter. Maslow's Hierarchy is a very valid framework. However, we also need peace, purpose, health, relationships, belonging (and acceptance) for a well lived life. For example, a large portion of people may say they go to work for a check, as if that is the only reason or reward, but it is not. Work, in and of itself, is its own reward. It holds its own intrinsic value. In this chapter, I will show the correlations between conversations and opportunities in a way that you may not have considered previously.

When I started to grow from (not leave), Corporate America, many advisors and consultants instructed me to use images from travels, cars, even check stubs to prove my 'success.' If that was not one of the most dismal periods of my life. In life we do want to present ourselves as credible, whether that's in business, with a new venture, as an authority in a certain field or within a certain discipline. However, check stubs as a reference just seemed dishonest *for me.* Maybe not for you, but for me, my core values and my reputation, those methodologies undermined the very credibility I was working to establish during my transition. Why? Because it was not my form. It was not the authentic Sharyn. *I don't do that.*

Holding your form in business is more than sticking to a business model or pricing structure. It is also the ability to hold your tongue in an opinionated world. This is increasingly difficult in our social media, information overload age. Be mindful of dead conversations, they lead to dead endeavors. When you are speaking with someone and you want them to view you as a credible business resource worth their time, their business, and their association; I want you to think about your conversation. If you are talking about another client or business competitor to a potential client, (even if you feel like you know and trust that individual), that is bad business. It is too familiar and will undermine *your credibility.* Often, we feel like we know the person and want their business so we speak to them relationally-but it is *based on the current relationship.* Here's the thing: although they may know you as a great person, they do not know you as a great *businessperson* yet. They really don't know that you are credible *in business.* You must speak to them based on the relationship you are developing NOW.

You may have gotten your real estate license and told all your closest friends, family, and colleagues; you are ready to shine yet no one is engaging you. You wonder: "Why won't they list their house with me?" It can be this simple: they don't know you as a credible real estate agent. They may know you as an alright person, a good mom, a nice member of the church- but they do not know you as a real estate person who can kill the game and get their house sold in a timely manner with minimal hassle. And so I ask, "Who are you talking to?" Because sometimes when we have those conversations, we get so familiar that we undermine the very component that we're wanting to reinforce -be it professionalism, articulation, savviness- whichever characteristic you want to convey and reinforce. We can undermine what we wish to build by being too familiar. If you are telling off color jokes with a potential client while they are attempting to talk about business, you are undermining what you are building. If you are gossiping about someone else, or about someone else's business, STOP. Quit kicking the ladder from underneath yourself. Recognize who you are talking to *and adjust.* Speak with the excitement of how many homeowners you're going to help, or of how many people you want to help achieve the dream of home ownership. Speak to the benefits of purchasing or selling a home in the current market. Who are you speaking with, and what relationship are you building?

Quit kicking the ladder from underneath yourself...Who are you speaking with, and what relationship are you building?

We spoke in relation to business but please note this also applies to career promotion. When you receive a promotion, who are you speaking to? If you get a promotion and now you are the Director/ Manager/ Supervisor, etc., *please, please, please*, do not talk about team members who report to you with other team members who report to you. I know that may be the person you are used to venting and debriefing with, it may be a former partner in crime, but it is irresponsible and professionally immature to speak about direct reports with other direct reports. As you navigate promotion, you will realize that emotional intelligence is worth more than technical skills for longevity and a healthy work environment. Choose the right audience. There are certain things that you will know, and you will be in the know about, that does not need to be communicated or shared with individuals who report to you.

You may think disclosing information about one direct report to another direct report is not a big deal. Allow me to share the progression of this practice. First, trust begins to erode. Trust takes time to build, and even *longer to re-build*. It also creates a disruptive workplace. If your workplace is a disruptive workplace because you don't know how to hold your tongue, then your upline and the decision makers are going to look at leadership, i.e., they are going to look at YOU. They will associate you with the dysfunction and toxic environment. For example, if your name is Angela, the decision makers may say, "When we placed Angela in a position of authority, stuff became crazy. We are having to devote more time to interpersonal firefighting because she doesn't know how to hold her tongue, and she doesn't know how to keep the confidences of her employees. She doesn't know how to manage confidentiality."

So, who are you talking to? Be aware of your audience, horizontally and vertically. The management practices you export will eventually boomerang back to you. As a leader, you are building culture everyday- even when you don't feel like it or think about it. Since you are building, you may as well build something you can live in, and with.

The management practices you export will eventually boomerang back to you.

When you apply for a promotion, who are you speaking to? Your upline is great and they know you're a solid worker, but they may not know you as a potential candidate in the role that you want to be considered for. So be aware of those conversations. Know your audience and know the conversation you're having with said audience. You may only get a moment or two to show your capability for the role you desire. Use those moments to demonstrate:

"I know how to be a decision maker. I'm decisive. I know how to problem solve. I have great engagement skills. I

know how to engage the staff. I know how to execute conflict resolution. I know how to bring people along as a team and foster a team environment, to uplift morale."

You may only have a moment, a brief window in time to communicate that to your upline. Length of relationship does not indicate depth of relationship. Your upline may have been around you 10 or 15 years and see you as a solid person. They may know you from countless company picnics or the company softball league. They may even know your children's names but the way they know you has not been as a decisive decision maker. Like the real estate example earlier; they do not know you as you want them to know you... *yet.* They may know you've got a decent set of morals, but they don't know that if they put you in a position that they can enjoy their weekend because you can handle whatever comes your way.

So, who are you talking to? Don't waste the conversation. The right conversation can change your trajectory. It can shift your life on the whole; it can change your income, your hours, your responsibilities, a conversation can increase your influence and push you into the next season of your life. Don't waste that moment. Don't waste those conversations. Stay authentic (people recognize fake a mile away) and maximize those moments.

You may only have a brief moment in time to communicate your willingness and ability to key decision makers.

Know who you're talking to; know what the conversation is about. *Know your audience.* Be Aware; be a problem solver. Bring solutions to the table. Don't ask questions like: "Did you know such and such is dating him or her?" "Did you hear about so and so's write up?" *No, no, no, no, no, no, no!* If you must do that, please have those conversations at your house with your significant other. But even then, you want to be mindful because holding items in confidence is critical to emotional maturity. When you can hold confidence, people recognize you as trustworthy and responsible. Trust is essential for credibility and holding your form can protect you from something that takes five seconds to say and five years to get over.

WAYTT Tip 1:
Ask Yourself: "Who Am I Talking To?"

When people bring you drama, ask yourself: Is the person I'm talking to able to help resolve this situation? Are they going to help perpetuate the drama? Is this conversation going to end here, or will I hear it again from someone I didn't share it with? Would I be embarrassed if somebody knew that I was engaging in this conversation? Is the person who is bringing this conversation to me likely to go tell somebody I'm co-signing even when I did not? Does this bearer of news have a history of gossip and messiness? *Who* are you talking to (*WAYTT*)? Who *are you speaking* with? Who are you *speaking for?* Identify who you are speaking to as far as people who report to you, who you're speaking with as far as your colleagues and who you're speaking with regarding applying for promotion. You will want to know your audience, you will want to be aware, and you will want to capitalize on those opportunities. Be mindful of dead conversations so you don't undermine the very thing you're trying to achieve, leaving you with dead endeavors.

CHAPTER 5

Failure and Disappointment

Letting Them Work FOR You

First, let's take a moment to celebrate. Breathe. We're here, some folks are not. Somebody else did not get to live this day. For this moment, I just want to encourage you. There's this quote, I think Bill Gates says it, "...success is a lousy teacher." It is saying success is not a good teacher because it may not adequately prepare us for adversity and adversity is inevitable.

I officiate basketball and it requires annual camps and testing to remain a certified official (able to work state sanctioned competitions). One year while at basketball camp, a fellow official had failed one of his medical school quizzes. Me, being the natural encourager that I am, began to offer comfort and rallying words of affirmation- 'so sorry to hear that, you will get them next time, etc.' I was really trying to encourage him, and he replied, "No, I'm glad I did." His response stunned me. He went on to explain, "I'm glad I did. If I would have not failed it, I wouldn't really know. I wouldn't have known what I'm doing wrong or what I wasn't strong in. Now I know. I don't want to have to guess when I'm working on somebody. If somebody's life is in the balance, I don't want to guess." Wow! I had never heard such a positive and insightful response to a failed test. He had not internalized that failure one bit!

Before my co-official shared that outlook with me, a failed test would at least have brought me some embarrassment. But now, not in the least. I recognize that failure is just another part of life. He saw failure in a much better way than I did; I had never really looked at failure from that perspective. I am very grateful that he didn't just say thank you to my encouraging words. His response was a gem in my life. Hopefully it will be a gem in yours too!

Stages of change

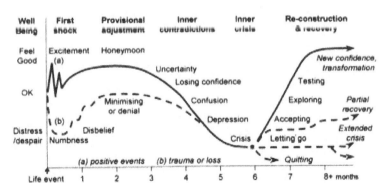

The transition cycle - a template for human responses to change (Williams, 1999)

When I share the Nuances of Leadership© with consultants, I often reference the stages of transition to demonstrate how and why people end up quitting the very jobs they worked so hard to get. It absolutely breaks my heart, because I know for many of the quitters it breaks their heart also.

Often people equate the stages of change with a major life event. Marriage, birth, death, divorce, moving, etc.; rarely however, do we focus on understanding HOW the changes affect mood, thoughts, actions, decisions, etc. If we did, we would better understand that the stages are not limited to major change only. Failure is not a major life change per say, but it does include specific stages associated with change- uncertainty, losing confidence, depression, etc. (see stages of change chart). For those who haven't learned how to process disappointment in a healthy way, it can create crisis. This is recognized in responses of quitting at the first no, or the first failed exam, or the first apology that wasn't received in a manner that we deem it should be received. Growth is not all or nothing, it is progressive. As is maturity. Quitting when things do not go the way you want is petulant at best, disastrous at worst. As the pastor next door would say, "Take another lap, Moses."

Regardless of our spiritual disposition, or lack thereof, the bible is a very widely read book. Within its pages, there is a fisherman named Peter that had to deal with public praise followed by public embarrassment, a quick temper and a devastating character failure that again was... public. Ouch.

But Peter's narrative gives us hope. Even though he failed at holding his form several times (and he had spectacular failures), he eventually got it together. Why? Because instead of continuing to run from crisis (disappointment, hurt, anguish), he began to understand these things are only final *if we allow them to be*. They are not the final authority, just stages, parts, segments, and seasons that will open into something better. When we understand this, it becomes easier for us to hold our form. Growth is progressive; and pain, disappointment and failure are inevitable components of it. Peter kept growing. As a result, he was one of the twelve men that turned the world on his head. He did not allow failures or disappointments to stop his growth, they helped *shape his growth* in a way that allowed him to stand and be stronger in his endeavors.

Focus on your goal and remind yourself of the successes. Take strength in your dream and stick with your game plan. *Adversity is not always an enemy*. It can be a coach, bringing out the best in you. Be willing to forego the short term, quick fix solutions to attain your long-term targets.

Progressive Practice Tip 4:
FACTS and the 3 Sheet Method

Sheet 1: What are the facts?

- ❖ *Is it valid?*
- ❖ *What can you do to change these facts?*

Sheet 2: Who...

- ❖ *Said it?*
- ❖ *Was there?*
- ❖ *Heard about it?*

Sheet 3: How...

- ❖ *Was it said?*
- ❖ *Did it look?*
- ❖ *Did it feel?*

After all questions are answered and explored; DISPOSE of sheets 2 and 3 and focus on Sheet 1 *only*. Do not revisit the second and third sheet.

Progressive Practice Tip 5:
Letting Disappointment Work for You

Disappointment is like pain and change- inevitable. It can be pretty disheartening, pretty discouraging and pretty painful. Yes. Especially the disappointments you just have to live with. Everything does not always come up roses, or even plain grass... But hold your form. Everything will come up.

I want to be as transparent as possible when discussing disappointment. When Hurricane Harvey hit Texas, we saw heartbreaking devastation, and we saw *how different people respond* to devastation. Some get critical and use their fingers and mouths to blame. Others go right to work, using their fingers and mouths to help. Some said it was the government's job to help, others said, "How can we help?" Whether we recognize it or not, these responses demonstrate the downward curve of the stages chart. HOW we handle crisis. Emotional maturity allows you to make an informed responsive decision without being reactionary and blaming. Solution over blame. When you experience disappointment or failure, look at the diagram and make an informed decision on which arrow you will follow.

Another way to disarm disappointment and minimize your time in it, is a simple statement I use to vet whether I may be about to over-respond. A fellow team member (we will call her Abi) said it to me when I was fussing and blaming a coffee shop for making me late. I felt it took them too long to give me my coffee! And I brought all of that negative energy right in the room with me! Abi looked at me fully, then very calmly stated, "And if that is the worst thing to happen to you today, you are having a good day." I wanted to be taken aback but it was so right I could just say, "Yeah." while nodding my head. Side Note: If you do not have one, get an Abi in your network, they are an advantage).

As part of Progressive Practice Tip 5, I want you to use this concept in question form. There is a difference between inconvenience and disappointment. Who cares if they didn't put enough ice in your drink? Or if you asked for light ice and they gave you more than enough ice. That is an inconvenience. Ask yourself: 'If this is the worst thing that happens to me today, am I having a good day?" More than likely, the answer will be yes. The right perspective is essential. Abi's statement refocused me that day. **A simple vetting process that keeps things in proper perspective while identifying the events and situations that may trigger, derail, distract, or otherwise result in an embittered mindset.**

Deal Breaker or Nah?
Is it a deal breaker? If yes, separate as appropriately as possible. If it's not a deal breaker, then prepare as best you can to navigate through the disappointment. I have experienced times of disappointment that included tears, feeling misunderstood, and well...*hurt*. Simple doesn't always mean easy and certain instances in my life were just not easy. There are times when disappointment is piercing,

and you feel it in the very core of your being. In your jaws, in the back of your eyes, in the back of your throat. I'm sure you have experienced the hot tears when things are really, really disappointing. I know you know what that's like. It is not pleasant, and it can feel very alienating. But you cannot stay there, friend. Process the pain, hold your form, and push through that space.

Trust that disappointment is certain to occur over the course of your life. It's inevitable, but it can work for you. It can make you look at something and say, "Alright, what could I do differently in this situation?" "Maybe that's not how it should have happened. Let's flip it around and see what can be done in a different way." It is also easy to get derailed when disappointment tears at trust. Don't let it stop you. Cry, ache, breathe-make sure you have a good support system in place. Fill your time with life-giving activities. Oftentimes when people are deeply disappointed, they begin to fill their time with things that aren't like giving. As uncomfortable as it is, as much as it hurts, as much as you don't feel like doing it, make yourself put yourself around things and people that are life giving.

Atmosphere Matters

Put yourself around the right people, and in the right places. This will encourage you even when you don't feel like you want to be encouraged. Feelings change, feelings are fickle, and they change. Picture a sleeping child when it is time to wake up for school. "Five more minutes," "I don't wanna get up..." because they do not *feel* like waking up or getting out of that warm, snuggly bed. Fast forward to 3pm that afternoon and that same child running through the door full of energy and stories about the day. "Mom, I had the best time at school! Ethan brought his brother's lizard for show and tell!"

This is a clear example of feelings changing. This can also be applied to our professional lives. There may be instances we don't feel like following the process. However, this is where emotional intelligence (holding your form) can serve even the newest leader. Here's the thing: you *feel* so many things when you are in certain stages. Feel it, feel the disappointment, cry if you need to cry, you know, if you need to work out, go work out. Do what you need to do to process that stage but don't stay there and don't allow transitional feelings to make permanent decisions. When you allow the feelings associated with transitional stages to dictate your decisions, you pause your flow and limit your growth. That stage becomes your ceiling until you have an opportunity to address that stage again.

When you allow the feelings associated with transitional stages to dictate your decisions, you pause your flow and limit your growth.

There are things that are going to dictate and influence our decision making. I am not saying we will never need to vent. We all experience frustration. However, with the ability to hold your form, frustration may influence a decision, but it is not allowed to make one. Hold your form. Process the emotions. Ask yourself, "Is this a deal breaker, is this a trigger, or is this is simply a misunderstanding that can build an even stronger relationship after an honest conversation?" Let disappointment and failure work for you!

CHAPTER 6

Overwhelm-ness

From Hospitals to Homework

"My husband needs, my wife needs, my kids need..." are words we hear every day before we even leave the house. Often before we even fall asleep the night before. Everyone needs something. It *can* feel like we are pulled in ninety different directions within ninety minutes. All of this before you've had your Monday morning coffee. You arrive to work to find freshly burning fires that the weekend has left for you. Some cases delayed, three physicians unhappy, and God forbid something was cancelled. Off to the races, you are- refereeing personality conflicts and mediating finger-pointing contests. You have not even touched *your workload,* meaning, *you* still have meetings with Infection Control, EOC, Risk Management, the Executive Team, and the list of vendors, suppliers, and various sale reps vying to get on your calendar. Good grief!

"Good Grief, Charlie Brown!"- Lucy

Working in healthcare, this could be the narrative of anyone connected to the Operating Room, especially in the fourth quarter of the year. Year-end volumes can rub at even the most proactive Perioperative and Sterile Processing Departments. Volumes begin to increase as patients begin to schedule procedures to accommodate insurance timetables. Although healthcare is the main example in this chapter, everyone has experienced being overwhelmed. Employees and family members must navigate back to school transitions, holidays, graduations, school expenses, wedding seasons- and through many more things that use our mental, physical and emotional real estate.

Life can be overwhelming *ANY* time of the year. We all have our seasons, and though I cannot (honestly) give you a 4-step plan to avoid it, I can share real time tips to help you navigate.

1. RECOGNIZE

"When feeling overwhelmed, we usually react by being frantically busy, by procrastinating, or by doing things clumsily or inefficiently... When a person is experiencing the paralysis of procrastination, he or she is suffering the pain and consequences of inner conflict. This pain is the product of helplessness, apathy, psychological paralysis, and a disconnection from one's intelligence, self, and will..." - Peter Michaelson

Something that often happens, yet is not readily acknowledged, is the fact that procrastination affects you *even when you are not the party that procrastinated*. This can create feelings of resentment, and sometimes an unwillingness to assist the habitual procrastinator, which may require usage of tips previously provided. However, that is not the focus here. □

The focus is recognizing when we are frantically busy. When overwhelmed, if you don't RECOGNIZE you are overwhelmed, the probability is you will remain in a state of overwhelm-ness. A state of off-the-cuff decision making, firefighting all the time, running from this to that- unable to maximize your time. RECOGNIZE this state. And then…

2. STOP

Take a breath. Take two minutes and just breathe. Once you recognize the feelings, emotions, and activities that come with "overwhelm-ness," take a moment. Take 5-10 seconds or 5-10 minutes to just clear your head. A clear head gives a clearer picture. Get a clear plan, make a clear checklist (whether you write it out with pen and paper, type it into your device, or speak it into your phone's voice recorder). Technology IS YOUR FRIEND. Although it may seem counterintuitive, the time you spend doing this *saves* you time and removes you from the proverbial hamster wheel.

NOTE: It is important to use clear and concise language when creating this list. Use the language that reflects how articulate and intelligent you are, and that will drive you towards the accomplishment of the listed items.

3. ANSWER THESE THREE QUESTIONS

I. *What needs to be done right now?*

Look at what you are/were doing. Is this going to help you accomplish what needs to be done today? If not, stop allotting time to it. Honor what needs to be done TODAY.

II. *What needs to be done this week?*

Follow the format for question 1 but line up the week instead of the day. After you prioritize the week (which may seem an eternity away), smile and get to work with question 3.

III. *Who/What will it involve?*

Will this involve other departments? Will you need to arrange/schedule a meeting room? Does it need to work around the surgery schedule? Who will reserve the room? Who will send out the invite?

These quick tips do not mean you will never be overwhelmed, flabbergasted, flustered or frustrated. It simply means you will not live there. Moments of being overwhelmed can in fact strengthen you emotionally, mentally, and spiritually. However, continual and extended periods of being overwhelmed are unhealthy at best, and destructive to personal relationships that are meant to bring life and refreshing.

Deadlines and due dates are a part of life, sometimes converging all at once. *Focus on what you can influence today.* And if you find yourself unduly irritated with your spouse, mad at your staff, and eating back to back pints of Ben and Jerry's- RECOGNIZE you may be overwhelmed. Breathe… and STOP. Deadlines should not be deadly.

Life is too short to miss.

CHAPTER 7

Going LEAN...

Permission to Say NO

Most times when people are overwhelmed, underwhelmed, or just worried about too many things, it is because their thoughts are ungoverned. Either the thoughts have gotten out of control, or they are no longer being monitored, but they are still setting the pace. Remember from THINK. On Purpose© *that our thoughts are designed to serve us, and not vice-versa.* In order for us to truly go lean and minimize waste in our thought life, and waste in our priority management, we must give ourselves permission to say "No." This chapter addresses going lean, permission to say No, and the hidden costs associated with being unable to say No.

Dr. Robert Rohm of Personality Insights asked, "What are you doing right now? And is it costing you?" Cost is not just associated with money. Cost includes time, energy, resources- not just financial, but emotional and creative resources as well. And then we have hidden costs. One hidden cost is the 'Unfulfillment Tax.' This is a tax your soul pays every time you deny or dismiss your 'calling' because you haven't been working on what you desire to work toward. Time is like money and attention; if you do not give it direction, someone else will. Part of holding your form is mastering the skill set of saying no. Often items on our calendar take up our time and use up our resources simply because we are not saying no. *No is a complete sentence.* There are things you want to do, things you know need your attention. Things you want to learn, areas you want to see grow. But if you continue to do things that are not connected to your calling, then that time will be used on something that is not actually beneficial. And you will continue to pay the Unfulfillment Tax.

No is a complete sentence.

But you do not have to. Jonas Gadson says, "When your value is clear, your decision is easy." Hold your form is a mantra that *helps your decision be easy,* and that applies in multiple areas of our lives. One is focus. For one whole year, we focused on the word 'focus.' Each week we discussed practical tools and systems to help maintain focus. Ensure that you have systems in place that can help you focus. Make sure that you have both internal and external systems that can help you be accountable while giving you honest and accurate feedback. It is okay to have an amen corner but since amen means so let it be; make sure your corner is amen-ing the practices and activities you wish to see more of. Les Brown says, "When things go wrong, don't go with them." You need people who are going to help you grow.

When things go wrong, don't go with them.
– Les Brown

There is a well-known quote that reads, "show me the five people around you and I'll show you your income."

This statement is not limited to income though. It also works with health, relationships, personal growth, spiritual growth, etc. you name it. You want your amen corner to have real time facts and information that can sustain what you're trying to build. Be mindful of what you share and with whom you share it. When you are re-prioritizing, going lean, and shifting into your solo business, your calling, or taking massive action investing in yourself, that is a very vulnerable time. Be sure that the counsel you are getting is sound and conducive *directionally*. The council should be focused on what is *best for you* from a possibility standpoint. Listen carefully to what is said, and whether it is possibility based or fear based. You cannot learn to swim from someone who is afraid of water. Invest in support systems that can keep you continuing towards your goals, that can keep you moving forward, rolling toward your desired end.

You cannot learn to swim from someone who is afraid of water.

These systems will cushion you from impulse buys... and impulse *whys*. Why am I doing this? It'll keep you saying, will this meet my goals? Will this meet our goals? Will this help me move forward in the direction I wish to go? Will it help us move forward? Will *what I am investing me in* advance me to the next phase, the next stage, or the next level in my business and career? These are real time questions that demand an answer. If you will take the time to answer these questions now, when someone else asks you to redirect your energies or de-prioritize your priorities, then you will be able to tell them no... *without an inordinate amount of internal guilt.*

Practice saying no, if only in a mirror, so you can also settle it in your mind and become more confident in valuing your time. Your response is the right response because it's not based on emotion-how they may or may not feel, or how you may or may not feel because you may be giving an answer they do not want to hear. It is you saying *yes* to something more valuable. Complete what you have already settled in your heart. Time does not replenish. Money does, energy does, creativity does; time is the only commodity that does not.

CHAPTER 8

Why 'Hold Your Form?'

Emotional Intelligence for the Masses

Years ago, I heard a fellow colleague sharing a story about her experience during a race within the sport of track and field. She was sharing about conditioning and how a lack of it resulted in people not 'holding their form' during their race (like my nephew Tim in the first chapter). Coaches often yell the term out to the track team members because the runners get tired and begin to lose their optimal running posture. Likewise, in life we get tired -maybe not in a physical competition- but mentally at work, spiritually we can get bogged down, or emotionally via relational interactions. We can all recall a time or person that served as an emotional vampire. There are so many ways that we can grow weary and when our conditioning is not in place or sufficient for the current situation, we cease to hold our form.

How do we hold our form? We remember not to get out of sorts because someone else is out of sorts, don't get out of whack because someone else is out of whack. When you hold your form, you keep the form that you desire, the form that serves you best. There is common adage that encourages people to fight fire with fire. Why? That only leaves everyone with a pile of ashes. Holding your form allows you to keep what you have worked (hard and consistently) for; you would not take a match to your endeavors, then don't let a quote such as 'fire with fire' make you burn up your efforts. Make sure that the form you are engaging with is the form you want. I'm going to give you three TRUE, REAL TIME scenarios and ways that you can hold your form.

In the first scenario, I was I was coming from a very promising meeting on my bike (I didn't have a car at that time). I came to a stoplight, thinking about the things that I had experienced in the meeting and something flew right in front of my face! It didn't hit me; it was just real close. I looked down and it was a potato; a brown potato! Puzzled, I look over my shoulder in the direction it came from and I see a car full of teenage boys laughing. I remember thinking, *'who just carries a random potato?'* The teenagers quickly drove off laughing, jeering, and pointing. I was livid!! What if that potato had hit me? And who gave them the right to throw potatoes at me? Immediately, I was like, "I may not have a car, but I do have a phone and I'm going to call 911 and give your license tag to the police." Just like that I forgot about the possibilities of the meeting and *allowed someone else to change my energy and focus.* Because *they* threw a potato, *I was about to* over-respond. Thankfully, I didn't call the police. They were teenagers; I've been a knucklehead teenager and I know some knucklehead teenagers, so I held my form. I breathed and asked myself: How do you want to spend the remainder of this evening? I chose to let it go, have a little mercy, and *to be intentional with my focus and energy.* Remember, I was in a great space when that potato came through, and that potato wasn't going to move me from focusing on promises and possibilities.

Triggers are real, and the sooner you know yours, the sooner you can remove the trigger's firing pins.

The second scenario with holding your form takes place in California, Berkeley to be exact. I was presenting THINK on Purpose during a conference. I happen to be in proximity to one of the evening speakers before she was about to speak. Just as she was preparing to step out of her room, someone comes to her with a situation that aimed to create chaos and it hit her...right in her emotions, right in her trigger. <u>MESSAGE:</u> Triggers are real, and the sooner you know yours, the sooner you can remove the trigger's firing pins.

Suddenly, this speaker was like, "I am tired of people taking advantage of me, I did everything I was supposed to do (which she had)!" Off to the races and down the rabbit hole! I literally had to say, *"hey, hold your form.* This isn't an emergency; it is only a distraction." Later she thanked me (she both would and has done the same for me). There are times when you must hold your form and pick your battles. The matter that was brought to her could have been handled at least three people removed from her. It was a distraction. She was ready, focused on the task at hand and almost let it get influenced negatively. *<u>It's imperative to have people who can speak to you and keep you focused when things get a little blurry.</u>* Holding her form allowed her to achieve optimal results in sharing the message she was there to share.

Do not get in the habit of accepting a no from someone who cannot give you as yes.

The last thing scenario I will share deals with tenacity...and faith. Both will be tested. A middle-aged former co-worker had a thyroid condition. She had lost her job and her insurance, but she needed the thyroid medication. Because she couldn't afford it, she ended up having a near death experience (the doctors called it a thyroid storm). After she was released from the hospital, the hospital sent her to a place in downtown Dallas. She went for the first visit and afterward said, "I don't want to go back there, they talk to people so rudely." Sometimes when people don't have control in their own life, they will try to exert control in other places. Hold your form, that's not about you unless engage that personality. Rarely does that personality have the final say. You do not want to get in the habit of accepting a no from someone who cannot give you as yes.

Wait for your yes. In the case of my coworker, she needed to get behind where that rude worker operated. I encouraged her to return. She was like, "No, she is not talking to me like that. I'm just not going to do it!" I said I understand (and I did). Then I asked if I could submit to her that: "a soft answer turns away wrath. Will you consider just going and understanding that this worker may say something rude and you can respond with 'This is what I need. Will you please help me?'" She said she would consider it. Well, she returned, and the worker was just as rude as before! However, this time my co-worker held her form and humbly asked point blank 'Will you help me?' She not only made it out of the overly full lobby area, the rude gatekeeper ushered her in to the decision maker and my co-worker ended up getting her medicine and all her doctor's visits covered for a full year! Yeah! Win for the form holding! That was enough time for my coworker's body and medication to regulate and return to a manageable space.

These three different stories demonstrate daily opportunities to develop our emotional maturity. When we hold our form, we are more able to see what we want come to fruition. You are not at the mercy of distractions, red herrings, wayward emotions, or knee-jerk reactions. This is the *WHY* of hold your form. Because it serves you *AND OTHERS.*

CHAPTER 9

Coach's Talk

Call to the HYF Movement

Listen, people get distracted and they don't even know they're distracted. They see shiny new objects or the latest technology and immediately begin to see where they can make it fit into their business or endeavor. I call it the shiny new object syndrome (SNOS). Different fields use different language, but it is a distraction. Finish what you started. Or you will end up with a bunch of shiny new objects and you don't even know how they work; let alone how they work together! Ungoverned SNOS is like a ship adrift without an anchor, drifting from one thing to the next. This results in you operating in something that was not your initial effort at all, possibly out in your gift or strength zone. Before you were trying to establish and implement your vision; now you are trying to emulate and imitate somebody else because looks good. No; hold your form and stick to your plans.

It is imperative to know *you*. If you don't know who you are, you're always going to follow someone else's dream. I subscribe to biblical principles and I'm a firm believer that if you don't know your call, you are going to answer someone else's. Get to know you. Your gifts, your strengths. Your gift will make room for you. Get to know you. Get to know what life is giving *for you*. Because if it's lifegiving to you, it will be life giving to the people you are to share it with. When you know and our focused on what you are called to do, it minimizes internal feelings of jealousy, insecurity, backbiting, cat fighting, and undermining. Additionally, you began to cover twice the ground in half the time.

If you are leading a team in Corporate America, or if you have just experienced your first promotion, I heartily encourage you to spend time getting to know your and your team's strength, and to invest in training on emotional intelligence. So you can hold your form and help them hold theirs.

It's emotional intelligence in its simplest form.

"In their Own Words"

Excerpts from Real Conversations

...with REAL People

Cynthia G., Entrepreneur, Optimal Organizer, Owner
Cynthia's Clutter

"I've been a student of Sharyn Combs for many years now. I've watched her share her knowledge on so many things. One of the items that really stands out to me is Hold Your Form. Who would have thought the words on a t-shirt- three simple words- *Hold Your Form*- would have an impact on my life and the way that I look and deal with people on an everyday basis in such a different manner? noticed that even in my everyday life I tend to share these ideas, thoughts and words of wisdom with my children, especially my daughter. What amazed me is that when I asked my daughter, "What do you think the words 'Hold Your Form' means?" -She had a totally different perspective on what it meant. However, I was really intrigued because it totally made sense. So, it led me to believe that Hold Your Form applies to everybody. Everybody can benefit and use these words in their everyday lives. Whether young or old, educated or not educated. Hold Your Form to me means *you don't always have to react the way that other individuals are reacting.* You can just do the things that you are comfortable with. You feel more comfortable of being receptive to other's ideas and things of that nature. I just love the fact that my dear friend associated me with this term, Hold Your Form. Absolutely great!

Sydney L., College Student
Rising Leader

Today my mama asked me a question about the saying, Hold Your Form. This is a saying that LaSharyn Combs came up with a while back. When my mom asked me this question, I was able to tell her my own testimony with this saying.

I'm a college student now and throughout college I was faced with a lot of challenges. I was able to use this saying through my everyday life. For example, whenever I was faced with a decision, and someone wanted to either sway my decision or infringe their opinion on it- I was able to tell myself in my head, Hold Your Form, your thoughts matter, what you're thinking about matters, don't let outside voices dictate what you're going to do with your decisions. Hold Your Form to me is something I try to hold on to and I use in my everyday life.

And it's something I try to give to my friends as well. Thank you.

Kathy R., Mother
Friend

Part 1

I'm Kathy Robinson, here's my short story of how I hold on and keep my form. Short story for me is I was married 27 years, 4 grown kids, lived in Tulsa all the time and I decided I needed to start over so I moved to Branson, MO and thinking that would be just a good start over well, it's been very hard, a lot harder than I thought it would be. Meeting people, finding a church, finding my way to Walmart, a lot of unknowns, out of my comfort zone totally. So, for me to hold on, I have to speak out loud, speak scriptures out loud, speak to myself out loud. I can do all things through Christ who strengthens me. I read the Psalms out loud, encourage yourself in the Lord like David did. I pray, it's hard for me to sleep at night so I'll just softly just pray out loud. When my head hears my voice speaking it goes into my head and into my heart. It blocks negative thoughts and the negative things that Satan would like to throw at me. Also, I like to do at least some exercise. I live on the fourth floor of an apartment, so I have to take my trash out, get my mail, that's exercise every day for me. I try to eat healthy just to keep myself in better shape. Then, do something nice for myself every now and then, for me I go and get my nails done. Just smile at people, you'll be amazed how it touches people and they smile back. You reap what you sow. Thanks Sharyn!

Part 2

I used to tell people about the Walmart automatic doors that you can sit in your car and look from a distance and hope that those doors are going to open and you can think or believe that they'll open but until you physically get out and start walking towards that platform and make them open they're not going to open. That's how I feel it is with life, if you want something to open, yes you can pray and ask God, but you need to physically go and do something. You've got to get out and walk towards those doors to have them open.

Angela D., Educator, Author, Speaker
CEO AMD Group. LLC.

Sharyn: Angela is the author of the book Focused, a dynamic book that can help you to track what you're doing and help you remained FOCUSED. It lines up with THINK. On Purpose's core principles to make sure that your thought life is on track and serving you instead of vice versa. I'm asking her today about the term, Hold Your Form. It's something that is not even that deep. It's pretty simple, but it applies in so many areas. I'm asking Angela, if she doesn't mind sharing a little about it, maybe the first time she heard it, what it means to her, how it's applicable in her life, if she's used it for her, or for others. Hopefully both but we'll just see what she says.

Angela: "So, the first time I heard, Hold Your Form, or that terminology was at church, I heard through you. It can mean a lot of different things, but I'll tell you what it means to me. When I think of Hold Your Form, and I think it's because of the time that I learned it and what I was going through spiritually that it was good for me. God was changing me and growing me in a lot of different ways; certain things that I used to do He was pushing me into another arena. For me, there was things He was like, "not anymore." And so, I was having to Hold My Form in certain situations, in certain conversations, different places, certain things that I would have done in the past I had to catch myself and Hold My Form. So, I think often as Believers when we begin to grow, and we can get to the point where we're in familiar situations. What do I do, how do I react? Do I do the same things that I used to do? You can have that dilemma and that's when I say to myself Hold Your Form, remember who you're representing. Remember that this life is no longer my own, I'm a new creation. I'm a new creature in Christ so I have to Hold My Form. Not in have to as in a taskmaster, but it's important to represent Jesus. So, I think about that and I think of it in a situation when I might resort to being in the flesh, I try to Hold My Form and be more like Christ.

In the same manner, I shared that with a family member, they were about to meet up with an old friend from high school, a person that they used to party with and this person has changed a lot and no longer doing certain things and I was like, "Hey, go have fun but just make sure that you Hold Your Form. Have a good time, but remember who you are... Hold Your Form."

Alester G., Educator, Entrepreneur, Artist
The Mathman!

"Yo, whassup whassup party people, it's the Mathman! I just want to tell my testimony and share a short story about a phrase that I heard from a special person, Ms. Sharyn Combs of UCDI- U Can Do It- Think on Purpose, Do Something Daily. Well, we connected, and we became partners, friends. She would say, in her stories, in her teachings that I had to tell myself to hold your form. Or she might throw that in there, 'be cool, hold your form.' You know, it wasn't anything that she was trying to tell me I should say, but I took notice, I heard it. I was like hold your form, so I thought what does that mean? I think it means stay cool, be calm, keep it together and go on through. ***Go on through.***

There would be times where pressure would be hot, circumstances be thick, ya know there's two seconds left on the clock and we need that payment and ya know I would always hear that phrase, hold your form. So since then, hold your form, came in the clutch for me because when the pressure rises and the anxiety rise, it's always keep it together, stay cool and go on through. And I can go even deeper than that because it grew into something even more, ya know what I'm saying, like woah, I didn't know it could get better than that, but yes it got better than that because I learned that if you are in an environment that is not conducive to your growth and is not helping you get to where you want to be.

I grew up in the projects and the projects kind of influenced a lot of people to do what the projects do. But I was fortunate enough to, we think of it as, make it out of the projects and get into college. Since then, I've traveled around the country, I haven't quite made it to around the world, but that's soon to come. They ask me how did you do that? What I learned is that what I was doing was synthesizing an environment within myself using my imagination. So, now that I understand that I synthesize environments. Let's say I synthesize this environment, this is my garage right, I mean it's kind of clean, but it's got a lot of stuff in it, instead of getting a storage I put it in my garage. You know that sometimes that clutter and stuff can be stressful. But listen, if you're in a stressful situation I learned that you can synthesize your environment by using your imagination.

Use your imagination to create an environment to inspire you, that makes you happy. You see yourself doing, being and having the good that you desire. Well, that environment that's making you feel and request or vibrate or vibe. So, when I learned that I created an environment for myself and I've become something more within myself that when I come out of that, the challenge is to Hold My Form. Ya know, the scripture say it like this, A man, he leaves the mirror and he forget who he is, and what he look like, ya know what I'm saying? Anyway, what I'm saying is when you create and synthesize an environment the goal is to Hold Your Form. Creative process 101. Listen, this is the MathMan and shout to my mentor, my coach, UCDI, U Can Do It."

Karen R., Accountant, Producer
K.O.A.R., Can I Play Sports

Hold Your Form. Hold Your Form are words that when someone has pulled in front of you in traffic and you want to curse them out. Hold Your Form is when someone crosses you or look at you crazy. Hold Your Form, it ain't that bad, you know, you don't always have to take the negative of things, you can take the positive. Just like you're having a bad day, they may be having a bad day. Hold Your Form, stay positive, stay focused, think on purpose. Hold Your Form, keep moving, don't let nothing stop you from your goals and the things that you're trying to accomplish. Hold Your Form, those are some great words that Sharyn Combs has allowed God to create in her- Hold Your Form, Think on Purpose, UCDI. Hold Your Form… those words are just ringing to me right now. Hold Your Form, it ain't that bad, and this too shall pass, Hold Your Form.

An example:
I'm on my way to the airport and have a flight. We started out in enough time, but you know when you're in another state you don't know about their traffic, their lines at the airport. Time became a crunch and it looked like I was going to miss my plane. I just stay composed, I held my form and didn't get mad at those in front of me, who were moving slow, they may not have been moving slow they might have moving right on pace, but because my time became a crunch it would've caused me to start reacting in a certain way, but I didn't. I held my form. I was holding

my form and I made it to my gate and the plane hasn't even started boarding yet. Just think if I would've start acting crazy because I didn't leave in enough time to make sure that I got to my gate, but I didn't. I held my form; I'm holding my form and it worked out for my good. Hold Your Form.

When I think of Hold Your Form, I think of holding your control. Control yourself, don't let yourself get outside yourself, don't wig out, don't go crazy -hold your form. Just like If someone jumps out in front of you on the road there may have been a time where you may have jumped out in front of someone else. So, you have to think about those things when you're tempted to get out of control or not hold your form. You have to think about, "Now have I done this before to somebody else?" Usually the answer is yes. That helps you stay humble and hold your form. When you think of the fact that I may have been the one that's done this to someone else and now it's happening to me, not as a payback, but it's just a way to control yourself, hold your form, *things happen, it's not totally directed at you,* it's just that things happen. Always practice holding your form.

Deronda L., Singer, Liaison
F.U.E.L., Beautiful Intelligent and Gifted

Q. When is the first time you heard Sharyn Combs of UCDI use the term Hold Your Form?

> A. I do remember the T-shirts that she came out with (the slogan) Hold Your Form. I don't even know that I put a lot of thought into it at first, but now I do find myself saying it to myself if I'm in a stressful situation with a deadline and I know that I can't get off track, so I use that for myself. If I'm being honest -when I'm playing games and I want to win and if I'm ahead I'm just saying hold your form, don't get distracted, don't lose concentration, don't let other people get you off center, just hold your form and you'll keep going the way you're going. So, I've often used it in games, for deadlines, for assignments, I just think it's one of those things that's just catchy, so you find yourself using it for different situations.

Q. Have you ever been in a situation where someone else was talking to you and you thought this would be a good time for them to hold their form?

> A. I don't know if I've thought those exact words, but I guess that's the same as when you see someone so anxious that you know that they're going to make a mistake and I often say, slow your roll. Just slow down, most situations are going to be the same ten

minutes from now as they are right now. Sometimes we just need to take a few minutes and think, so it will still be the same scenario, hold your form, think for a minute, you have time, don't rush. Often most of our mistakes come from rushing, because of fear, anxiety, somebody is going to beat us to it. So, whatever it is, hold your form, be still for a minute, slow your roll, you've got time. So yes, I've often been in conversations with people and thought that.

Q. Is there anything else that comes to mind when you think of Hold Your Form? Any way that you think it would apply or encourage someone else to use it?

A. I just think because it is such an easy saying and if you get in the habit of holding your form, I do think sometimes before we make comments or snapbacks on people that we often try to make, if the thought is there, just hold your form. I do think it would keep us from moving unnecessarily or saying things or doing things. People used to say just count to ten. That's a form of holding your form. Whatever would slow you down enough to think the situation through before you react, respond, make suggestions, that's it, that's what I think- Hold Your Form. See, I'm holding my form right now, no need to keep adding to when nothing needs to be added! ⁂